AF437385

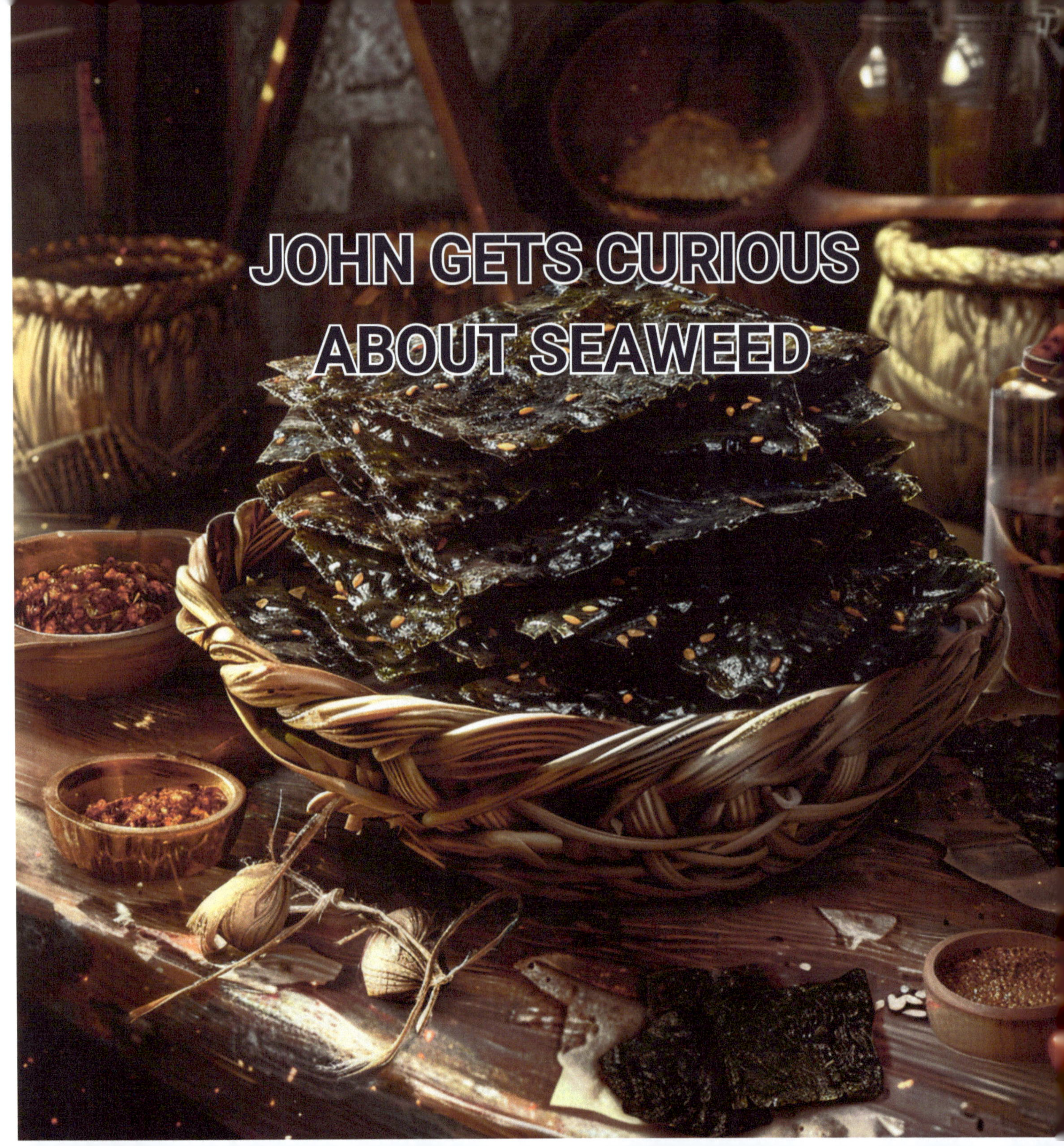
JOHN GETS CURIOUS
ABOUT SEAWEED

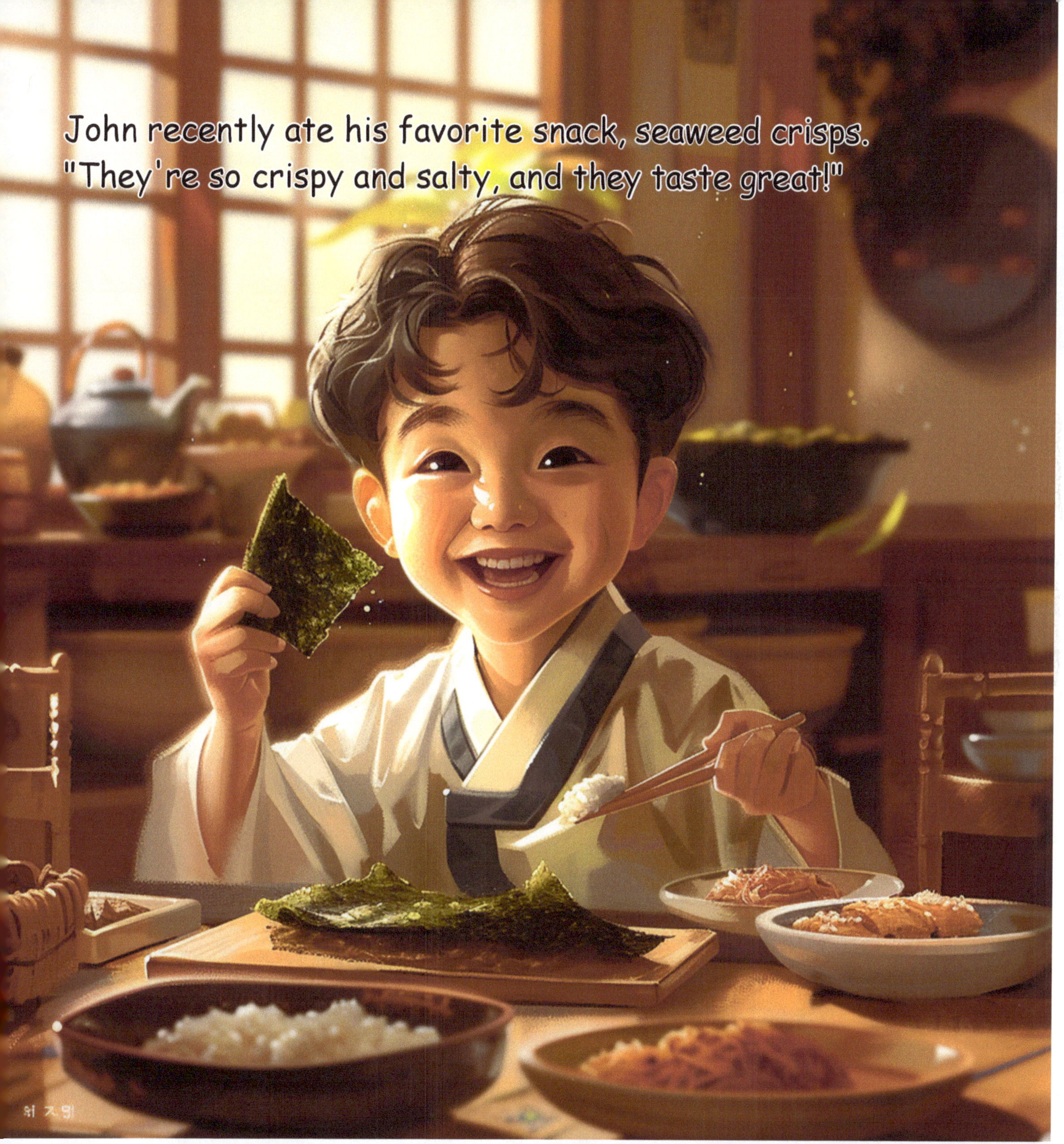
John recently ate his favorite snack, seaweed crisps.
"They're so crispy and salty, and they taste great!"

Seaweed is delicious in sushi rolls, and it tastes good in
salads or other dishes too.
John got curious about how seaweed is made.
So he asked his teacher, and this is what he found out.

How Seaweed is Made
Seaweed, the main ingredient of seaweed snacks, is harvested from the sea.
In the past, people used to pick seaweed one by one from rocks, but now, it is mostly farmed. There are two farming methods: pole cultivation and floating cultivation.

Pole Cultivation: This traditional and eco-friendly method is used in shallow waters with big tides. Poles are fixed to the sea bed, and nets are tied to these poles to grow the seaweed.

Floating Cultivation: This method doesn't use poles. Instead, nets are floated in deeper waters with smaller tides. To prevent other seaweed from attaching, the nets are flipped every four days.

After harvesting, the seaweed is taken to a factory.
In the factory, the seaweed is washed with clean water to remove any impurities.
Then, it is dried in large dryers and roasted over fire.
This process enhances the flavor and aroma of the seaweed.

The finished seaweed is made into various products like seasoned seaweed, seaweed snacks, seaweed sauce, and salted seaweed, and then sold.

The Nutritional and Health Benefits of Seaweed
Seaweed is low in calories and rich in nutrients, offering many health benefits.

Vitamins

Vitamin A: Helps protect vision and boosts the immune system.

Vitamin C: Prevents cell damage and strengthens the immune system.

Vitamin E: Contributes to skin health and prevents aging.

Vitamin K: Important for blood clotting and bone health.

Minerals
Calcium: Necessary for strong bones and teeth.
Iron: Essential for producing red blood cells and transporting oxygen.
Magnesium: Helps with muscle and nerve function, blood sugar control, and protein synthesis.
Iodine: Supports thyroid function.

Seaweed also contains plant-based protein and dietary fiber, which improve digestion and prevent constipation.

The Environmental Sustainability of Seaweed
Seaweed is called a "blue food." Blue foods are foods that come from the sea.

Seaweed absorbs carbon and helps combat climate change. It also uses very little water, fertilizer, or pesticides, minimizing its negative impact on the environment.

Seaweed farming protects marine ecosystems and provides habitats for marine life.

Seaweed improves water quality by absorbing nitrogen and phosphorus, reducing ocean pollution.

John learned that the seaweed he loved to eat was not only tasty but also nutritious and good for the environment. This made him love seaweed even more!

honglee books recommended books

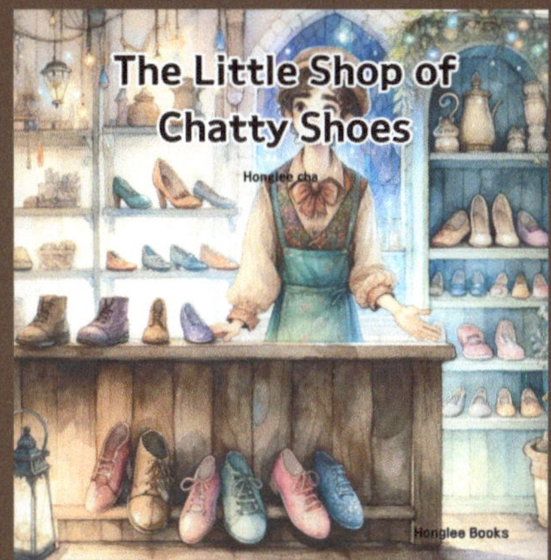

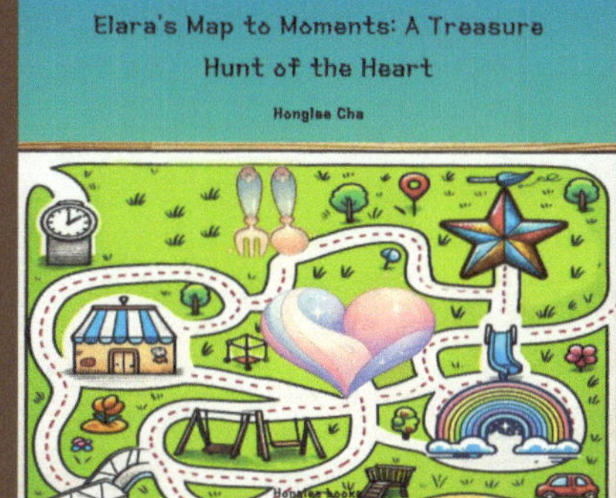

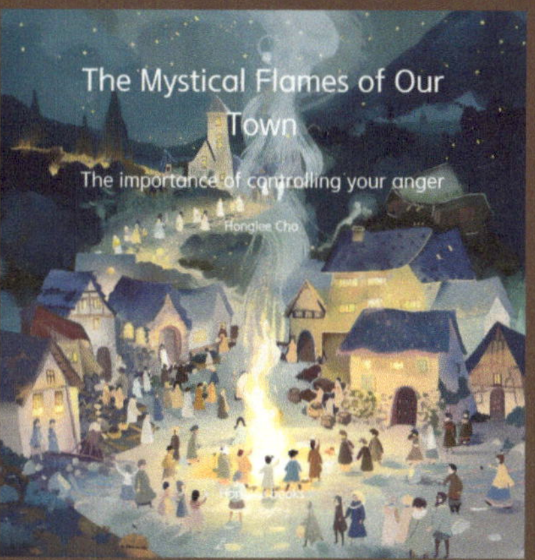

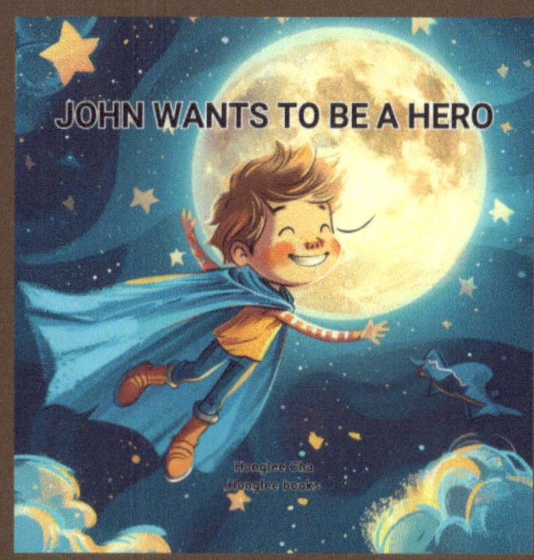

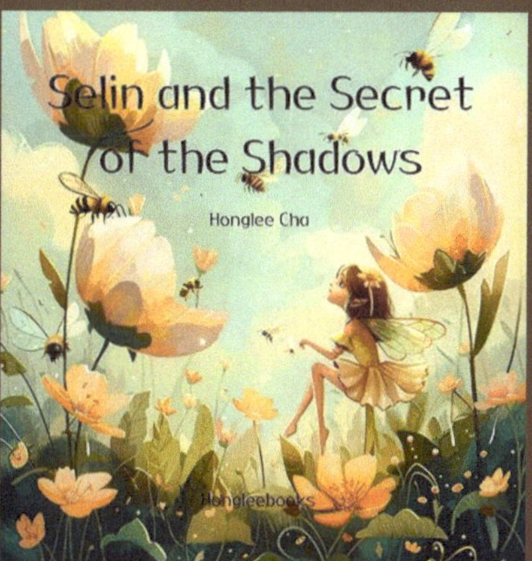

honglee books recommended books

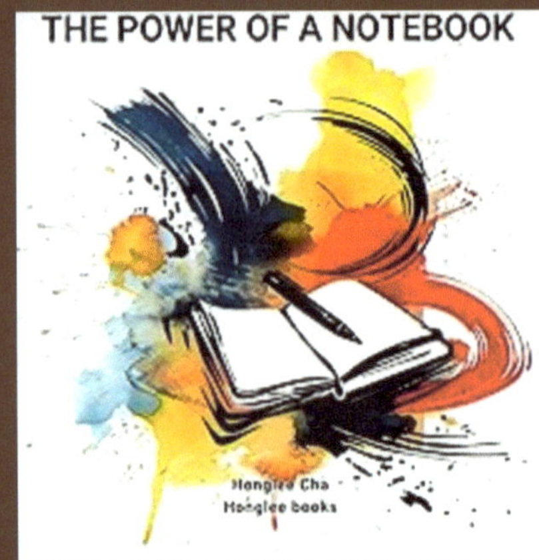

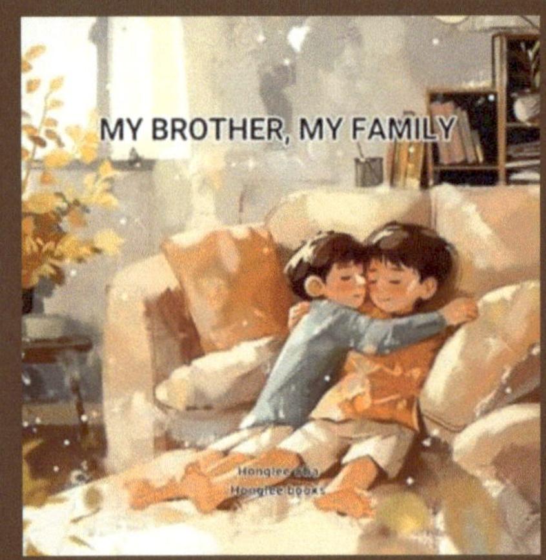

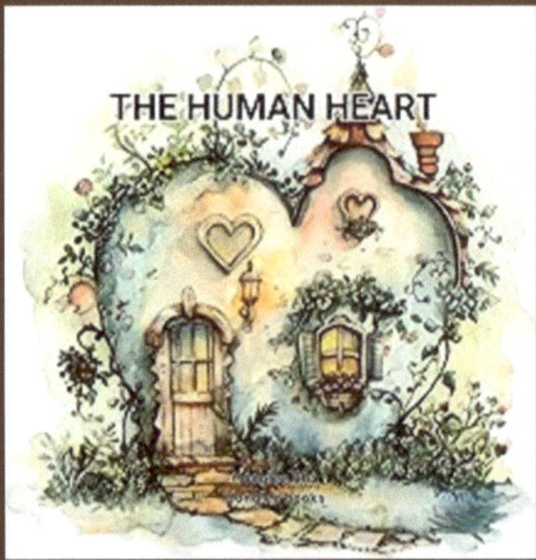

honglee books recommended series

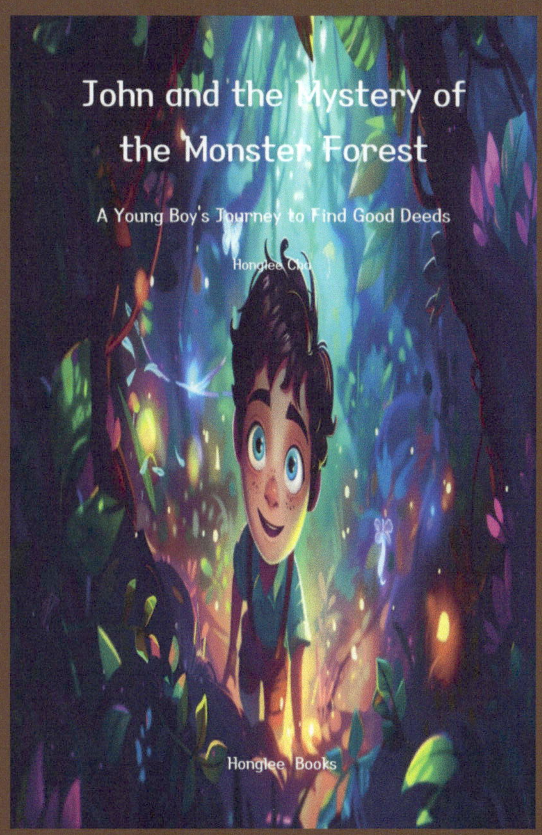

john mystery story

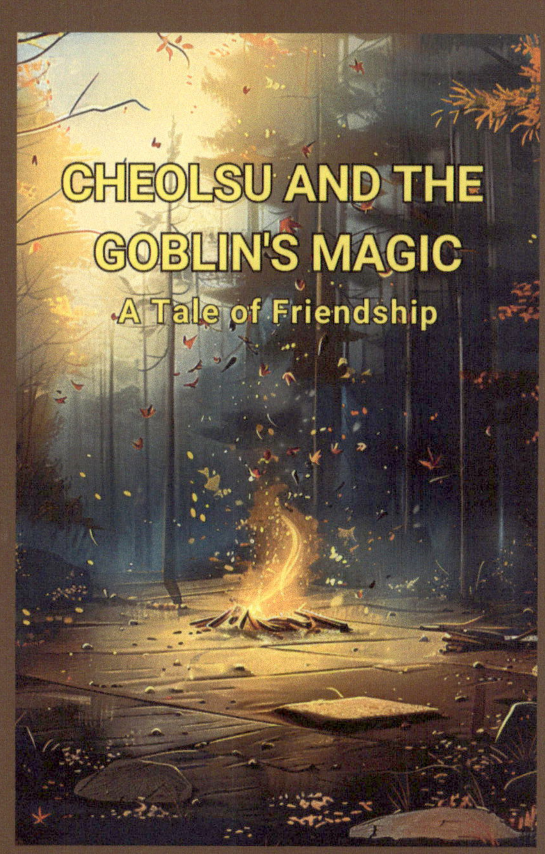

Cheolsu special story

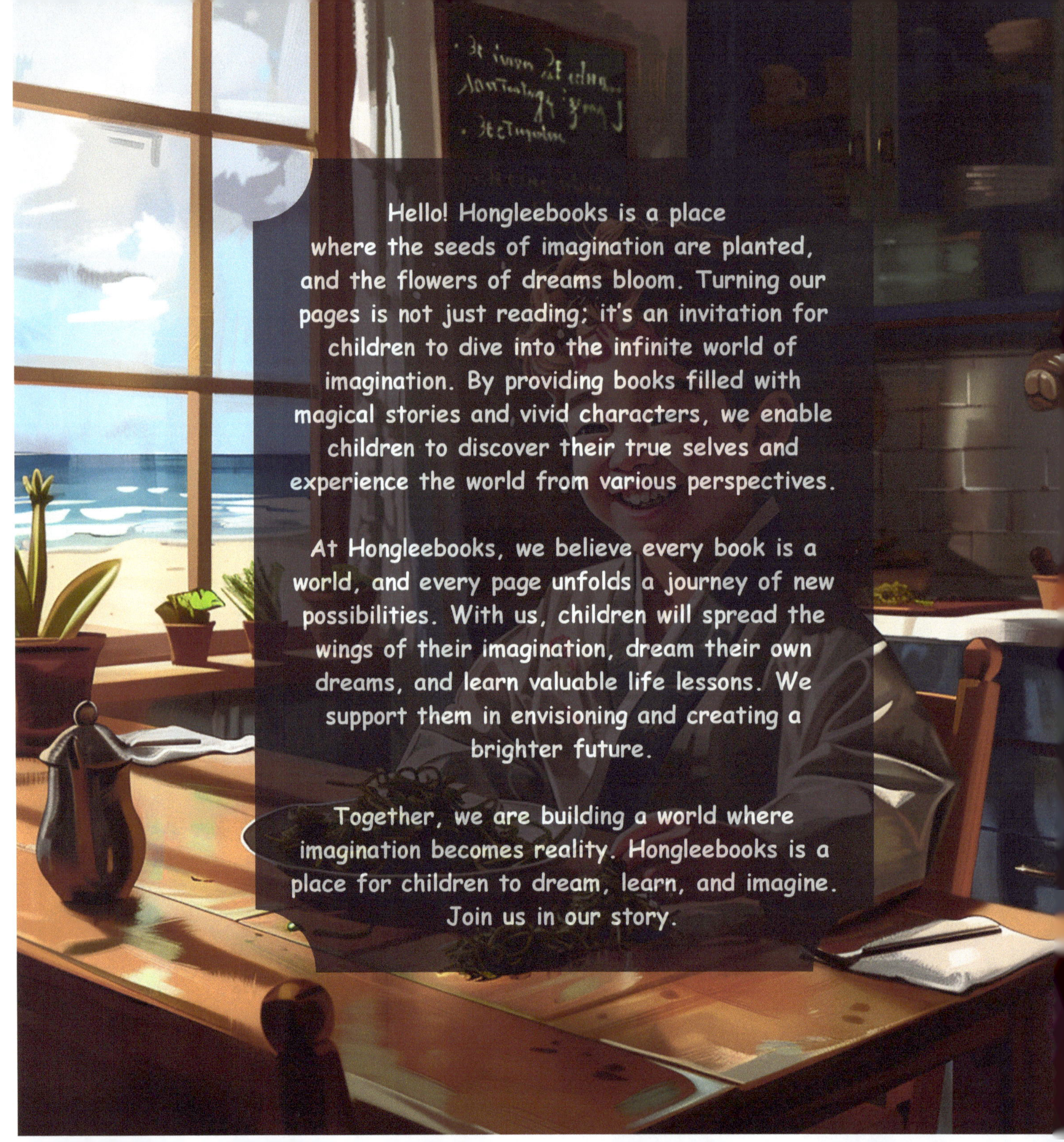

Hello! Hongleebooks is a place
where the seeds of imagination are planted,
and the flowers of dreams bloom. Turning our
pages is not just reading; it's an invitation for
children to dive into the infinite world of
imagination. By providing books filled with
magical stories and vivid characters, we enable
children to discover their true selves and
experience the world from various perspectives.

At Hongleebooks, we believe every book is a
world, and every page unfolds a journey of new
possibilities. With us, children will spread the
wings of their imagination, dream their own
dreams, and learn valuable life lessons. We
support them in envisioning and creating a
brighter future.

Together, we are building a world where
imagination becomes reality. Hongleebooks is a
place for children to dream, learn, and imagine.
Join us in our story.